J-E
HAL

Hall, Kirsten.

My trucks.

$17.50

DATE			

My Trucks

Written by Kirsten Hall
Illustrated by Patti Boyd

My First
READER

children's press®

A Division of Scholastic Inc.

New York Toronto London Auckland Sydney
Mexico City New Delhi Hong Kong
Danbury, Connecticut

Library of Congress Cataloging-in-Publication Data

Hall, Kirsten.
  My trucks / written by Kirsten Hall ; illustrated by Patti Boyd.– 1st
American ed.
       p. cm. – (My first reader)
Summary: While a little boy plays with his toy trucks, he imagines
driving various real trucks, such as a fire engine, a farm pickup, and
an ice cream wagon.
  ISBN 0-516-22935-4 (lib. bdg.)   0-516-24637-2 (pbk.)
  [1. Trucks–Fiction. 2. Toys–Fiction. 3. Imagination–Fiction. 4.
Stories in rhyme.] I. Boyd, Patti, ill. II. Title. III. Series.
  PZ8.3.H146Mye 2003
  [E]–dc21
                              2003003643

1 2 3 4 5 6 7 8 9 10 R 12 11 10 09 08 07 06 05 04 03

Note to Parents and Teachers

Once a reader can recognize and identify the 41 words
used to tell this story, he or she will be able to read successfully
the entire book. These 41 words are repeated throughout the story,
so that young readers will be able to easily recognize
the words and understand their meaning.

The 41 words used in this book are:

a	fast	love	truck
ahead	fight	mail	true
all	fire	my	two
and	for	on	up
around	garbage	red	way
car	get	room	you
come	I	stuck	you'll
day	if	the	your
do	I'll	there's	
dream	inside	to	
drive	is	tow	

I love to drive!

I drive a truck.

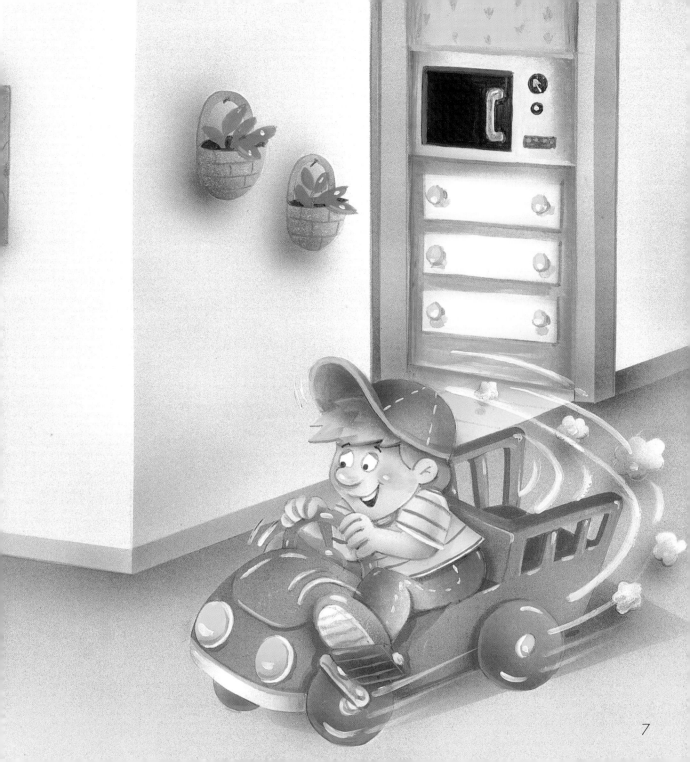

I'll tow your car if you get stuck.

10

I'll drive my truck

around all day.

I'll get your garbage on my way!

15

16

My fire truck is fast and red.

I'll fight the fire up ahead!

19

I drive a truck.

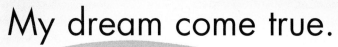
My dream come true.

23

Inside my truck is mail for you!

I love to drive my truck. I do!

You'll love my truck.

There's room for two!

ABOUT THE AUTHOR

Kirsten Hall has lived most of her life in New York City. While she was still in high school, she published her first book for children, *Bunny, Bunny.* Since then, she has written and published more than sixty children's books. A former early education teacher, Kirsten currently works as a children's book editor.

ABOUT THE ILLUSTRATOR

Patti Boyd has been an illustrator for more than thirty years. She lives in Jackson Hole, Wyoming, where she has been actively involved in the business and nonprofit community since 1980. She enjoys hiking, wildlife watching, and her new grandson.